W9-DJD-230

ACTION MATH
MEASURE

Ivan Bulloch

Consultants
Wendy and David Clemson

WORLD BOOK
in association with
TWO-CAN

2 What Size Is It?

Every day we ask questions such as:
How big is it? How tall is it?
How heavy is it?
What time is it?
All of these questions
have something to
do with measuring.
In this book we will
be looking at lots of
different ways of
measuring.

We use words such as *big* and *small,*
tall and *short,* or *heavy* and *light* to
describe things around us.

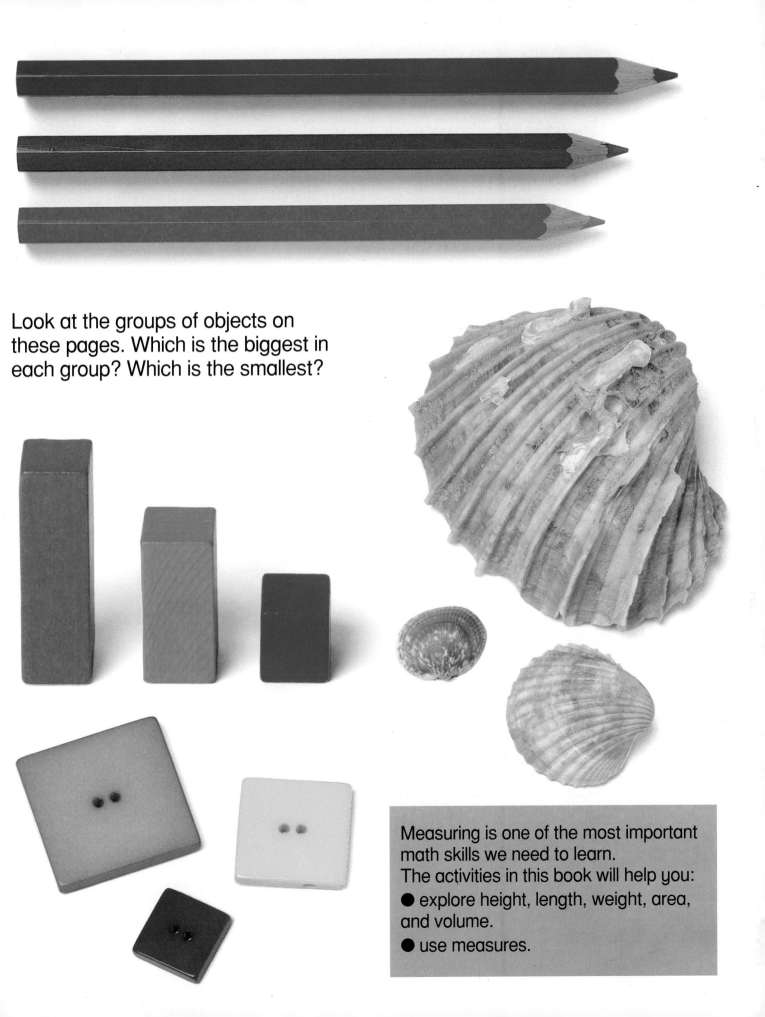

Look at the groups of objects on these pages. Which is the biggest in each group? Which is the smallest?

Measuring is one of the most important math skills we need to learn.
The activities in this book will help you:
● explore height, length, weight, area, and volume.
● use measures.

4 **How Tall Are You?**

Make your own height chart so that you can measure yourself.
● Glue or tape several large pieces of colored paper to make one long strip that is taller than you are.
● Use a building block to make equally spaced lines down the side of the paper.

Colored Strips
● Use a ruler and the block to measure strips of colored paper. The strips should be the width of your chart and the height of your block.
● Cut out the strips carefully.
● Glue one strip along the bottom of your height chart. Leave a space and glue another strip between the second and third lines from the bottom. Keep gluing equally spaced strips until you reach the top.

Here's what you learn:
● how to make and use measurement.

● Hang the chart on a wall so that the bottom touches the floor.

● Stand next to your chart and ask someone to make a mark on it right over your head. Count the number of strips from the floor up to the mark. Now measure your friends against your chart. Who is the tallest? Who is the shortest?

● Measure yourself and your friends again in one month. Has anyone grown taller?

6 Puppet Play

How big is your hand? Here is a way to make a hand puppet that will fit you like a glove!

Make a Pattern

🔴 Put one of your hands flat on a piece of felt. Draw a mitten shape slightly larger than your hand on the felt.

🔴 Cut out two mitten shapes exactly the same size. You could use different colors for the back and front.

🔴 Place one felt shape on top of the other. Ask an adult to help you sew all around the edge, except across the bottom. Use brightly colored thread to sew the pieces together.

● Now you are ready to decorate your puppet. Can you guess what these puppets are going to be? Turn the page to find out.

Here's what you learn:
● how to investigate area.
● how to compare sizes.
● how to match shapes.

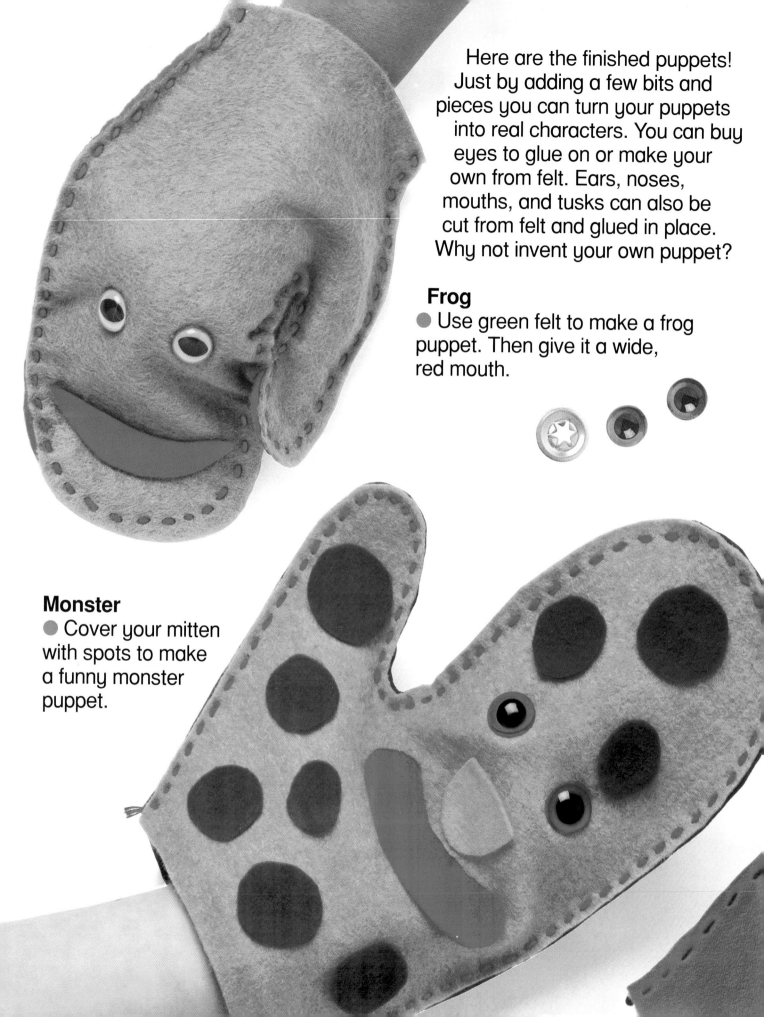

Here are the finished puppets! Just by adding a few bits and pieces you can turn your puppets into real characters. You can buy eyes to glue on or make your own from felt. Ears, noses, mouths, and tusks can also be cut from felt and glued in place. Why not invent your own puppet?

Frog
● Use green felt to make a frog puppet. Then give it a wide, red mouth.

Monster
● Cover your mitten with spots to make a funny monster puppet.

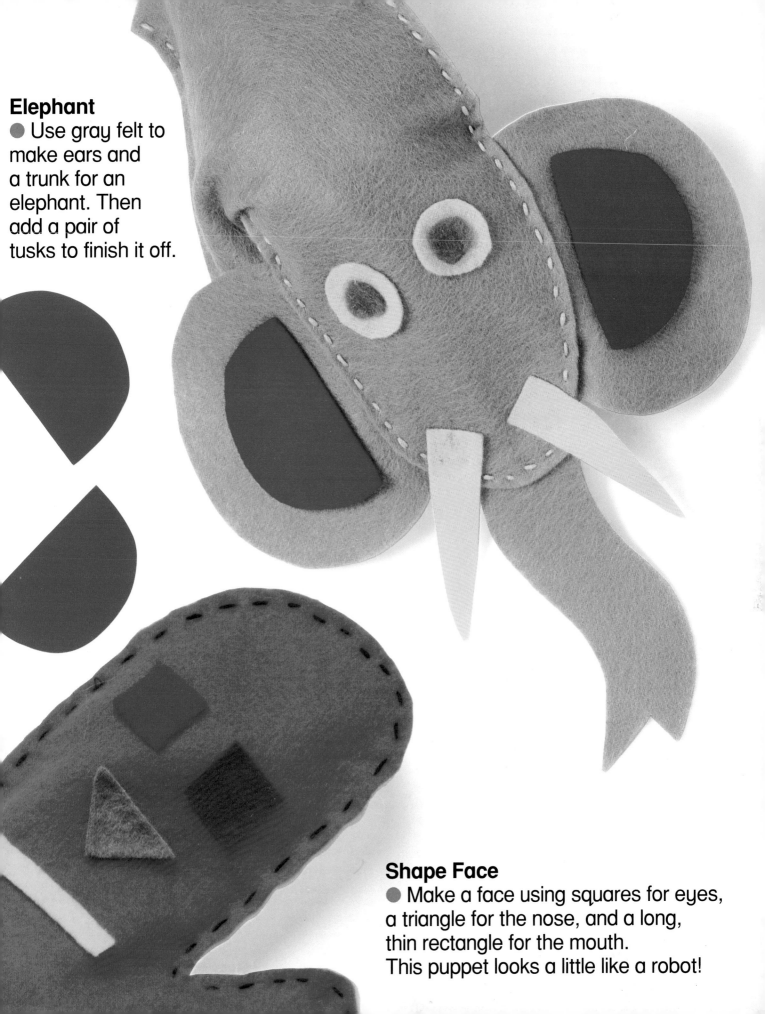

Elephant
● Use gray felt to make ears and a trunk for an elephant. Then add a pair of tusks to finish it off.

Shape Face
● Make a face using squares for eyes, a triangle for the nose, and a long, thin rectangle for the mouth. This puppet looks a little like a robot!

10 Finger Puppets

Here is an easy way to make a puppet that will fit on your finger.

Bird

- Cut out a small paper circle. Make a cut from the edge into the center.
- Fold the paper around to make a cone and tape the edge.
- Tape the cone onto the paper tube.
- Cover the paper tube and cone with several layers of paste and pieces of torn newspaper. You can make your own paste by gradually mixing water and flour until the mixture is thick and creamy.

Making a Tube

- Take a long strip of paper or thin cardboard and wrap it snugly around your finger.
- Tape the end and then gently pull the tube off your finger.

● When your puppet is dry, you can paint it. Why not make a puppet to fit every finger?

Sombrero

● Make a tube that fits your finger, as you did before.

● To make the sombrero, cut out a paper circle. Ask an adult to help you make some small slits in the center of the circle. Push the circle over the paper tube to make the brim of the hat.

● Cover the tube and brim with newspaper and paste as before.

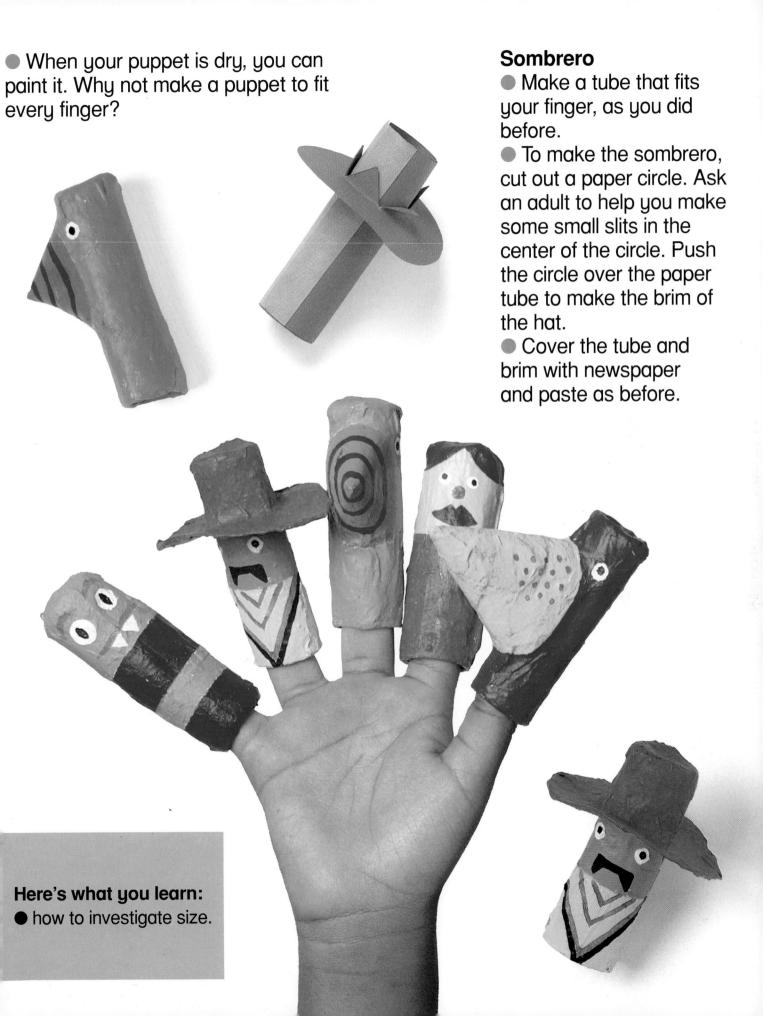

I2 Cutout Mask

We used a paper plate to make our mask. You will need to know where to make holes for your eyes, nose, and mouth. Here is a good way to take the measurements.

Measure It Out

● To measure the distance between your eyes, hold a piece of yarn in front of your face, stretching from the middle of one eye to the middle of the other. Then, lay the yarn in the middle of your mask and mark each end.

● Next, measure the length of your nose. Stretch a piece of yarn from the middle of your eyes to the bottom of your nose. Use the yarn to mark the mask.

● Finally, stretch a piece of yarn from the bottom of your nose to the middle of your mouth and mark it on the mask.

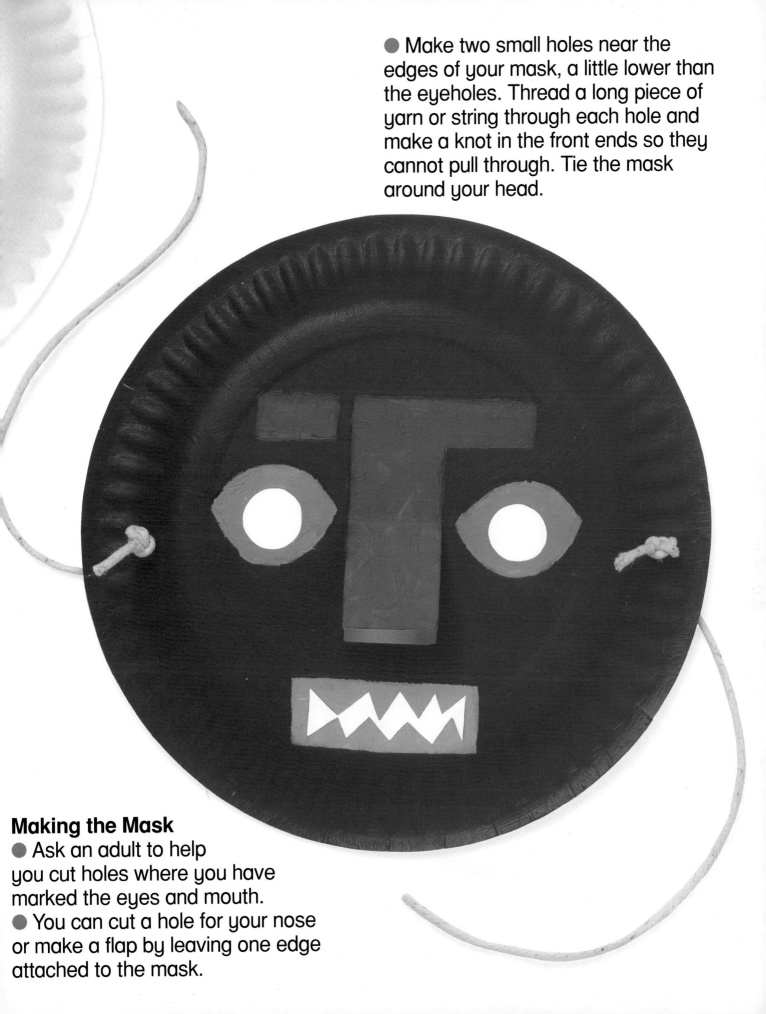

● Make two small holes near the edges of your mask, a little lower than the eyeholes. Thread a long piece of yarn or string through each hole and make a knot in the front ends so they cannot pull through. Tie the mask around your head.

Making the Mask
● Ask an adult to help you cut holes where you have marked the eyes and mouth.
● You can cut a hole for your nose or make a flap by leaving one edge attached to the mask.

Once you know how to make a basic mask, you can make up all sorts of different ways to decorate it.

Tiger

● First, paint a striped tiger face on your mask.

● Next, cut out some paper ears, paint them, and glue or tape them to the top of the mask.

Bird

The feathers on this bird mask are made from paper.

● Cut feathers of different sizes.

● Glue the large feathers on first and the smaller ones on top of them. To make the beak, cut a piece of folded paper. Unfold it and glue it in place.

Here's what you learn:
● how to use measurements.

16 Paper Dolls

Here is a way to make a cardboard doll and a whole wardrobe of paper clothes. First, draw the outline of a person on cardboard or trace around the doll shown below. Ask an adult to help you cut it out. Then, make some clothes…

Making a Shirt
● Place the doll on colored paper and draw around the top half of the body.
● Lift the doll off and draw a shirt shape slightly larger than the doll's body.

● Draw two tabs on the top of the shirt at the shoulders. Ask an adult to help you cut out the shirt. Put the shirt on the doll and bend the tabs over to hold it in place.

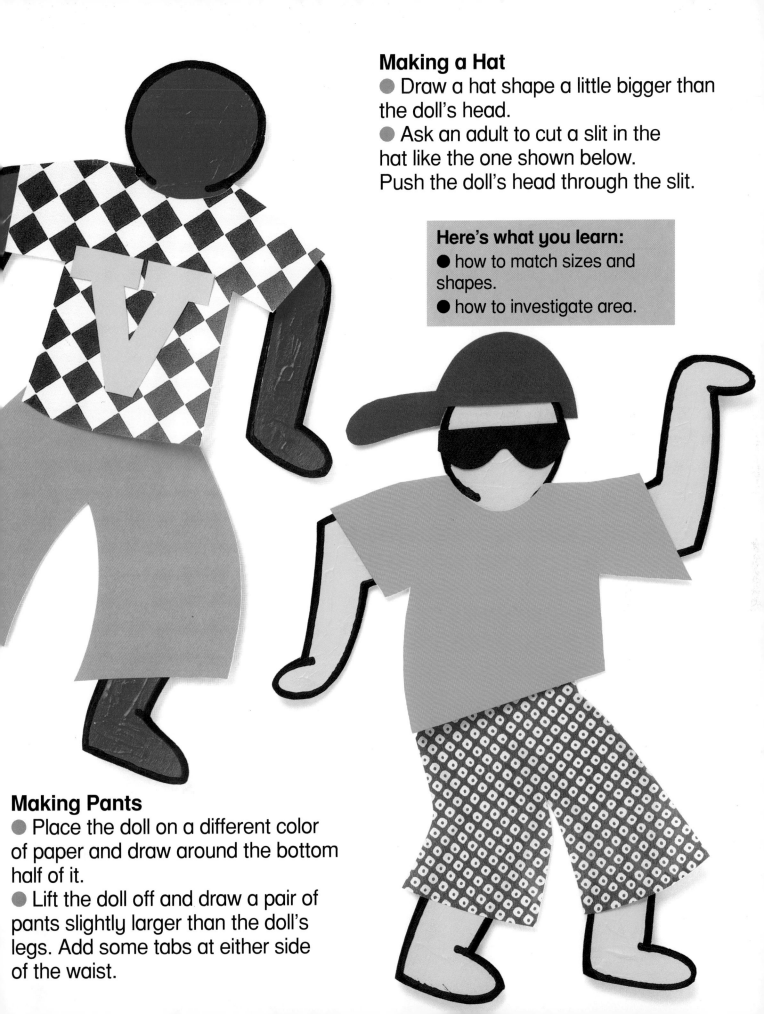

Making a Hat
● Draw a hat shape a little bigger than the doll's head.
● Ask an adult to cut a slit in the hat like the one shown below. Push the doll's head through the slit.

Here's what you learn:
● how to match sizes and shapes.
● how to investigate area.

Making Pants
● Place the doll on a different color of paper and draw around the bottom half of it.
● Lift the doll off and draw a pair of pants slightly larger than the doll's legs. Add some tabs at either side of the waist.

18 Bottle Band

It is hard to believe, but you really can make your own band with some empty glass bottles, water, a metal spoon, and a plastic cup to use for measuring.

● Make a mark about a quarter of the way up an empty plastic cup.
● Fill the cup with water up to the mark. We added a little food coloring to the water to brighten up our bottle band.
● Pour the water from the cup into the first bottle. You may need a pitcher or a funnel to help.

● Pour two measures from the cup into the second bottle.

● Now pour three measures into the third bottle, four into the fourth bottle, and five into the fifth bottle.

● Play your bottle band by knocking gently on the sides of the bottles with a metal spoon.

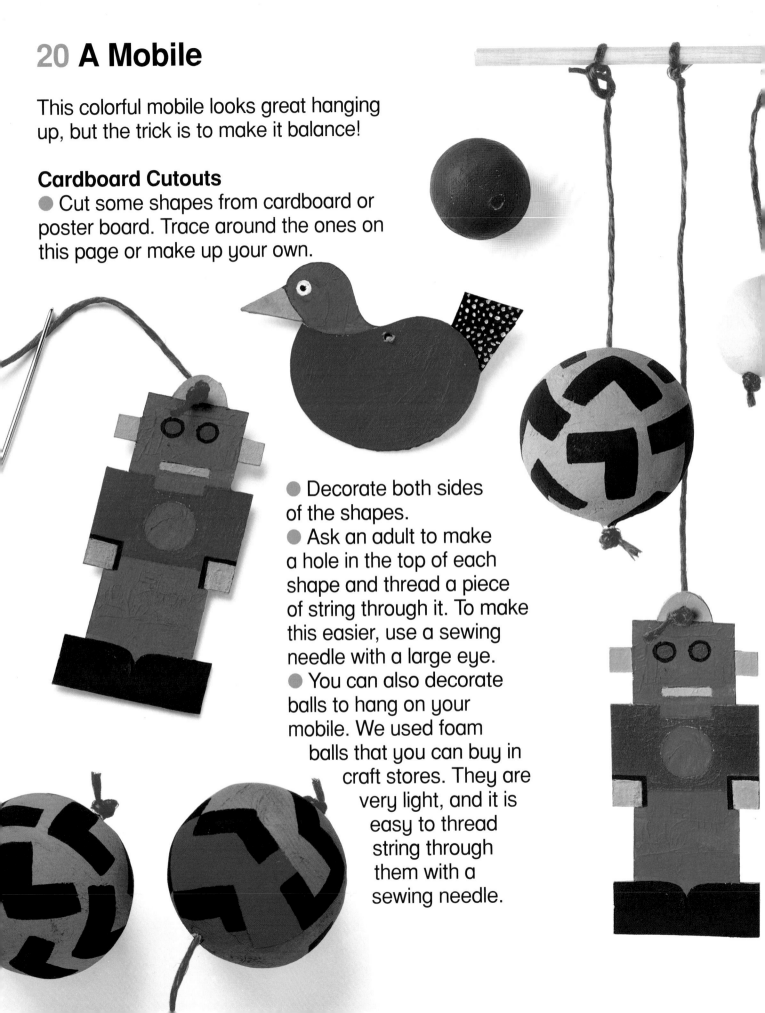

20 A Mobile

This colorful mobile looks great hanging up, but the trick is to make it balance!

Cardboard Cutouts

● Cut some shapes from cardboard or poster board. Trace around the ones on this page or make up your own.

● Decorate both sides of the shapes.
● Ask an adult to make a hole in the top of each shape and thread a piece of string through it. To make this easier, use a sewing needle with a large eye.
● You can also decorate balls to hang on your mobile. We used foam balls that you can buy in craft stores. They are very light, and it is easy to thread string through them with a sewing needle.

Hang It Up
● Attach a piece of string to the middle of a long stick or dowel. Use this string to hang your mobile.

● Tie the objects to the stick in different places. Slide them along the stick until the mobile balances. You may also have to adjust the lengths of the strings so that the objects don't touch each other.

Here's what you learn:
● about weight and balance.

22 Baking Cookies

It's very important to measure carefully when you are baking. Ask an adult to help you measure the right amount of each ingredient.

You Will Need:
3/4 cup all-purpose flour
1/4 cup granulated sugar
1/3 cup butter
2 drops vanilla extract

● Ask an adult to heat the oven to 325°F.

Mix It Up
● Put the flour and
sugar into a mixing bowl.
● Cut the butter into small pieces
and add it to the bowl. Use your
fingertips to rub the butter into
the flour. (Make sure your hands
are clean!)
● When the mixture looks like
fine bread crumbs, add the vanilla
extract. Use your hands to
make the mixture into a large
ball of dough.

Roll It Out
● Press the dough on a surface lightly
sprinkled with flour.
● Use a rolling pin to roll the dough
into a thin, flat shape that is about the
same thickness as a coin.
● Cut shapes using a cookie cutter.
● Put the cookies on a greased cookie
sheet and bake them for 20 minutes.
● Ask an adult to take the cookies out
of the oven. Use a spatula to put the
cookies on a wire rack to cool.

Here's what you learn:
● how to use standard
measures.

24 Cookie Boxes

When you have made your cookies, you might want to give some away as a present. Here are two ways of making boxes in which to pack them.

Pile Them Up

● Put one of the cookies on a piece of cardboard. Using a ruler, draw a square slightly bigger than the cookie. Cut out two squares exactly the same size. These will be the top and bottom of the box.

● Decide how many cookies you want to give away and pile them up. Stand a piece of cardboard against the pile to measure the height. Make a mark on the cardboard.

● Use a ruler to draw a cardboard rectangle slightly taller than the pile of cookies and the same width as the square you have already cut out. Cut four rectangles this size. These will be the sides of the box.

● Tape the bottom and sides together. Put the cookies in the box and tape the last square on top to make the lid.

Spread Them Out

● Lay six cookies flat on a piece of cardboard and draw a rectangle around them. Cut out two rectangles that size.

● Cut four thin strips of cardboard—two the same length as the rectangle and two the same width as it.

● Tape the strips to the rectangle to make the sides of the box.

● Tape the other rectangle on top to make the lid.

Here's what you learn:
● about area and volume.

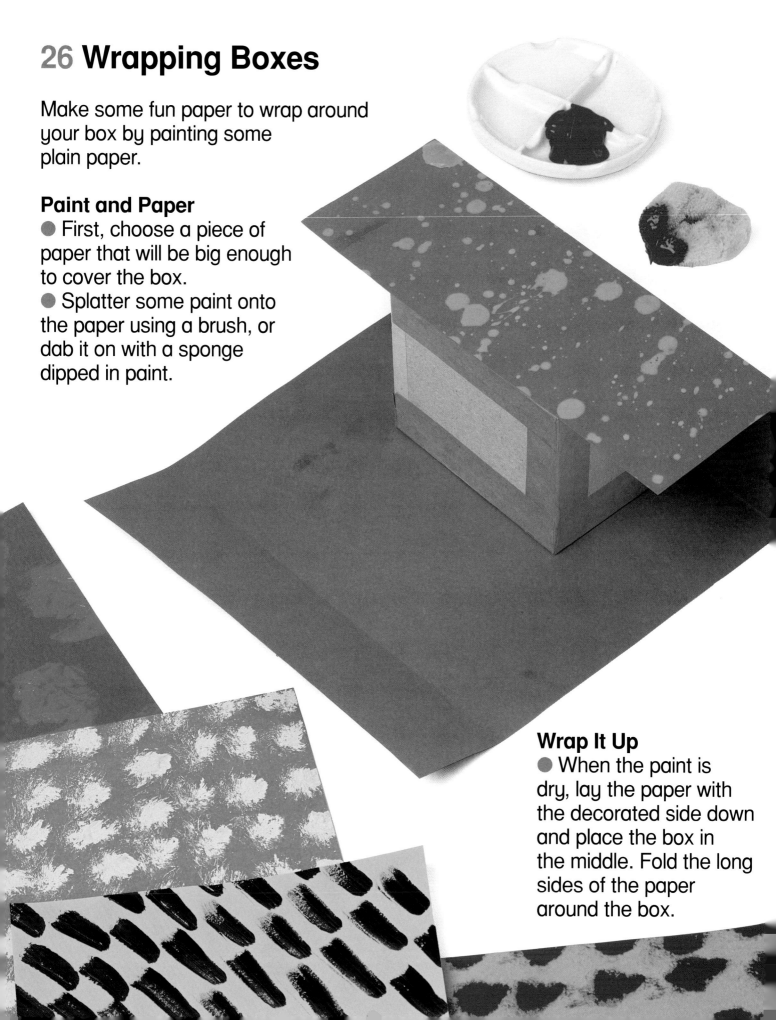

26 Wrapping Boxes

Make some fun paper to wrap around
your box by painting some
plain paper.

Paint and Paper
● First, choose a piece of
paper that will be big enough
to cover the box.
● Splatter some paint onto
the paper using a brush, or
dab it on with a sponge
dipped in paint.

Wrap It Up
● When the paint is
dry, lay the paper with
the decorated side down
and place the box in
the middle. Fold the long
sides of the paper
around the box.

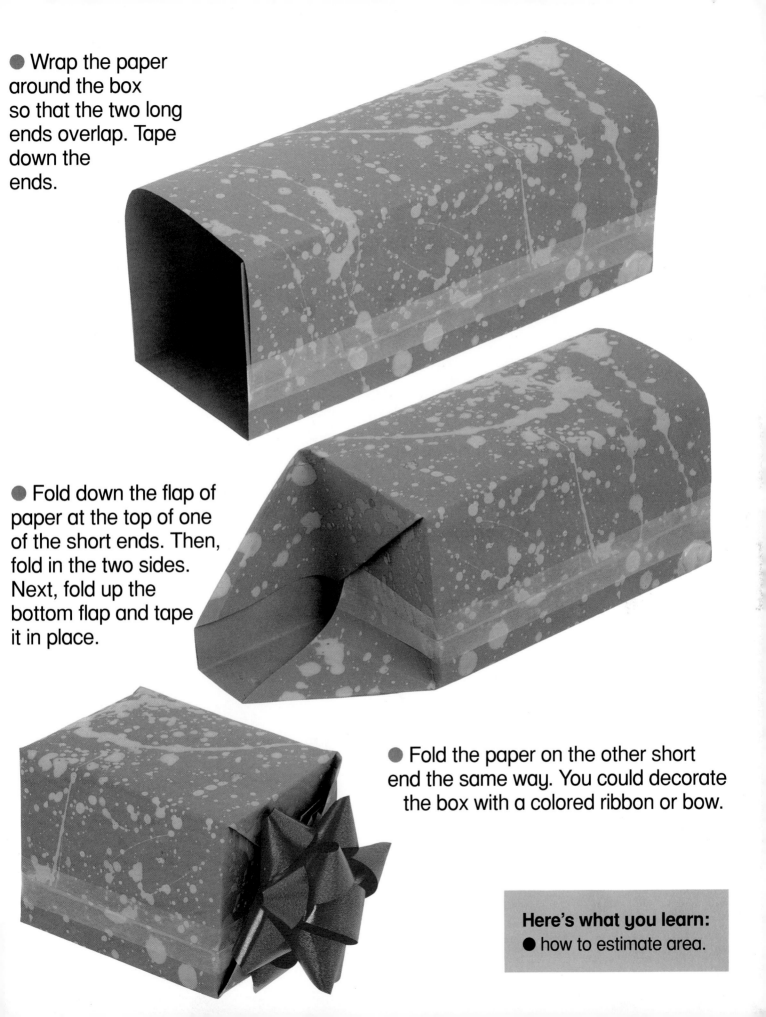

● Wrap the paper around the box so that the two long ends overlap. Tape down the ends.

● Fold down the flap of paper at the top of one of the short ends. Then, fold in the two sides. Next, fold up the bottom flap and tape it in place.

● Fold the paper on the other short end the same way. You could decorate the box with a colored ribbon or bow.

Here's what you learn:
● how to estimate area.

28 **Sand Timer**

Here's a way to measure how much time something takes.

Paper Cone
● Draw a big circle on a piece of poster board. You could trace around a big plate.

● Cut out the circle. Then, ask an adult to help you cut a slit from the edge of the circle to the center.

Here's what you learn:
● how to measure time.

● Fold one side of the slit around the other to form a cone shape, like the one below. Tape it in place.
● Cut a tiny hole in the bottom of the cone.

A Line of Triangles
● Cut out several paper triangles all the same size. Glue them in a line up the side of an empty bottle.

Falling Sand
● Place the cone in the top of the bottle and fill it with sand. Watch the sand fall through the cone and fill up the bottle. The sand gradually reaches each triangle mark.
● Have a friend watch your timer while you hop around the room. How many marks does the sand pass? Does your friend take the same amount of time to hop? What else can you time?

30 Tangrams

A tangram is a square that has been cut into seven special pieces. The pieces can be put together to make different patterns or pictures. Look at the pictures shown on this page and the next. Can you find a small square and five triangles in each picture? The black shape is called a parallelogram. It is also in all of the pictures.

Making a Tangram
● Ask an adult to cut out a square from thick cardboard.
● Use a ruler and pencil to mark the shapes shown above.

● Cut along the lines and paint each piece a different color.

● How many pieces make up the tangram? Mix them all up. How many pieces do you count now?

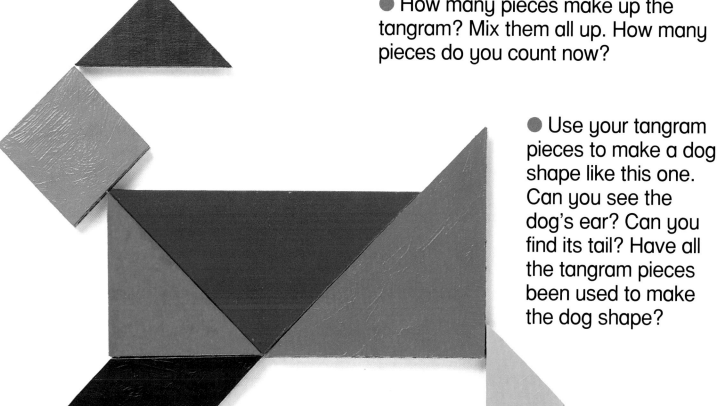

● Use your tangram pieces to make a dog shape like this one. Can you see the dog's ear? Can you find its tail? Have all the tangram pieces been used to make the dog shape?

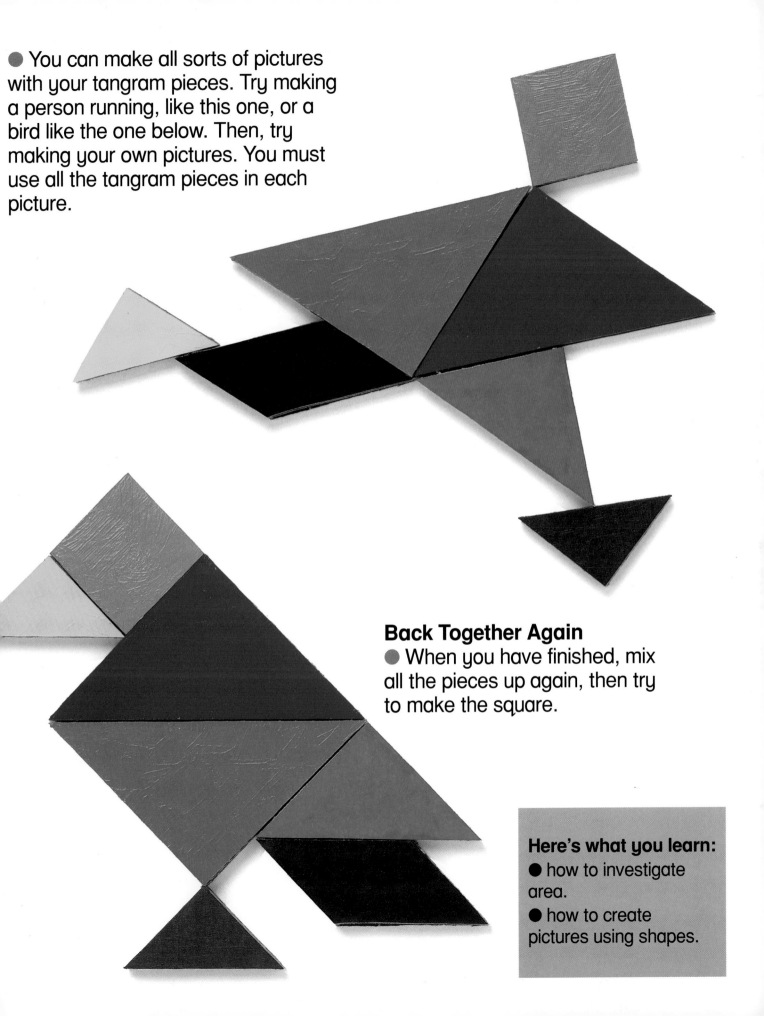

● You can make all sorts of pictures with your tangram pieces. Try making a person running, like this one, or a bird like the one below. Then, try making your own pictures. You must use all the tangram pieces in each picture.

Back Together Again
● When you have finished, mix all the pieces up again, then try to make the square.

Here's what you learn:
● how to investigate area.
● how to create pictures using shapes.

Editor: Diane James
Editorial Assistant: Jacqueline McCann
Design: Beth Aves
Photography: Toby
Text: Claire Watts

Published in the United States and Canada by
World Book, Inc.
525 W. Monroe Street
Chicago, IL
60661
in association with Two-Can Publishing Ltd.

**For information on other World Book products,
call I-800-255-I750, x 2238,
or visit us at our Web site at http://www.worldbook.com**

**Library of Congress
Cataloging-in-Publication Data**

Bulloch, Ivan.
    Measure / Ivan Bulloch; consultants, Wendy and David Clemson.
        p.   cm. – (Action math)
    Originally published: New York: Thomson Learning, 1994.
    Includes index.
    Summary: Teaches simple measuring techniques such as estimating,
counting, and sorting by means of various handicrafts.
        ISBN 0-7166-4906-3 (hardcover)—ISBN 0-7166-4907-1 (softcover)
        I. Mensuration–Juvenile literature.   [I. Measurement.
2. Handicraft.]   I. Clemson, Wendy.   II. Clemson, David.
III. Title.   IV. Series: Bulloch, Ivan.   Action math.
QA465.B89   1997
530.8–dc21   96-49797

Printed in Hong Kong

2 3 4 5 6 7 8 9 10 0I 00 99 98 97

Skills Index

Consultants
Wendy and David Clemson
are experienced teachers and
researchers. They have written
many successful books on
mathematics.